DESERT
Food Webs

By William Anthony

BookLife PUBLISHING

©2019
BookLife Publishing Ltd.
King's Lynn
Norfolk PE30 4LS

All rights reserved.
Printed in Malaysia.

A catalogue record for this book is available from the British Library.

ISBN: 978-1-78637-624-4

Written by:
William Anthony

Edited by:
Madeline Tyler

Designed by:
Jasmine Pointer

All facts, statistics, web addresses and URLs in this book were verified as valid and accurate at time of writing. No responsibility for any changes to external websites or references can be accepted by either the author or publisher.

Nottinghamshire Education Library Service	
E220187906	
Askews & Holts	Oct-2019
577.16	£12.99

Photocredits:
Images are courtesy of Shutterstock.com. With thanks to Getty Images, Thinkstock Photo and iStockphoto.

xpixel (sand texture), YamabikaY (paper texture). Front cover – Gary L. Miller, arka38, Eric Isselee, wacpan, sma1050. 2 – Milan Zygmunt. 3 – Eric Isselee. 4&5 – Clari Massimiliano. 6 - 99Art, Adisa, Maciej Olszewsk. 7 – Nicholas Taffs, Alexander Wong, Don Mammoser. 6 & 7 – JaySi. 8 – Justin Buchli. 9 – Pacific Northwest Photo, Pedro Alvera, Public Domain, https://commons.wikimedia.org/w/index.php?curid=338979, Natalia Kuzmina. 10 – Stephen Mcsweeny. 11 – Audrey Snider–Bell, Ikhwan Ameer, Elliotte Rusty Harold, rorue. 12 – Nicholas Taffs. 13 – Been there YB, Maria Uspenskaya, Charles T. Peden, http://www.birdphotos.com (CC BY 3.0 (https://creativecommons.org/licenses/by/3.0)), from Wikimedia Commons. 14 – Charles T. Peden. 15 – Charles T. Peden, Pedro Alvera, Ali Iyoob Photography. 16 – Protasov AN. 17 – wacpan, acceptphoto. 18 – Charles T. Peden. 19 – irin–k, Julie A. Curtis. 20 – Max Allen.

CONTENTS

Page 4 In the Desert
Page 6 The Food Web
Page 8 The Red-Tailed Hawk
Page 10 The Rattlesnake
Page 12 The Kangaroo Rat
Page 14 The Grasshopper
Page 16 The Scorpion
Page 18 The Cactus Longhorn Beetle
Page 20 The Kit Fox
Page 22 Desert Food Web
Page 24 Glossary and Index

Words that look like THIS can be found in the glossary on page 24.

IN THE DESERT

Go on a walk, see the incredible sights... but be careful! Do you know who might be hiding underneath the rocks, looking for a nibble?

There are lots of different animals and plants to be found, all going about their daily business, and each and every one of them has a place in the food web.

Let's look at who-eats-who in the desert. What can we find in the deserts of North America?

THE FOOD WEB

It all starts with the Sun's energy...

...HERBIVORES eat the plants...

...which feeds plants...

THE RED-TAILED HAWK

Never forget to look up. While everybody goes about their business on the ground, I'm flying through the skies looking for my next meal. I'm an apex predator, so I've got a big menu of <u>PREY</u> animals to choose from...

NAME:	Red-Tailed Hawk
TYPE:	Bird
HOME:	North America
FOOD:	Carnivore
PREDATOR OR PREY?:	Apex Predator

So many options down on the desert floor, but what do I go for?

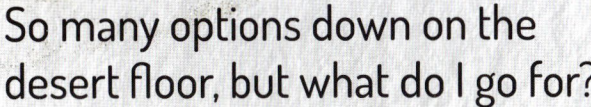
Jackrabbit: big but brilliant...?

Kangaroo rat: jumpy but juicy...?

Grasshopper mouse: small but super...?

No, none of these are making my tummy rumble. I think I'd prefer something scaly...

WHO HAS SCALES? →

9

THE RATTLESNAKE

Hisssss. Don't let that hawk know that I'm ssslithering around down here. I'm so hungry. Although I'm not an apex predator, there are still lots of meals on my menu. But what do I want?

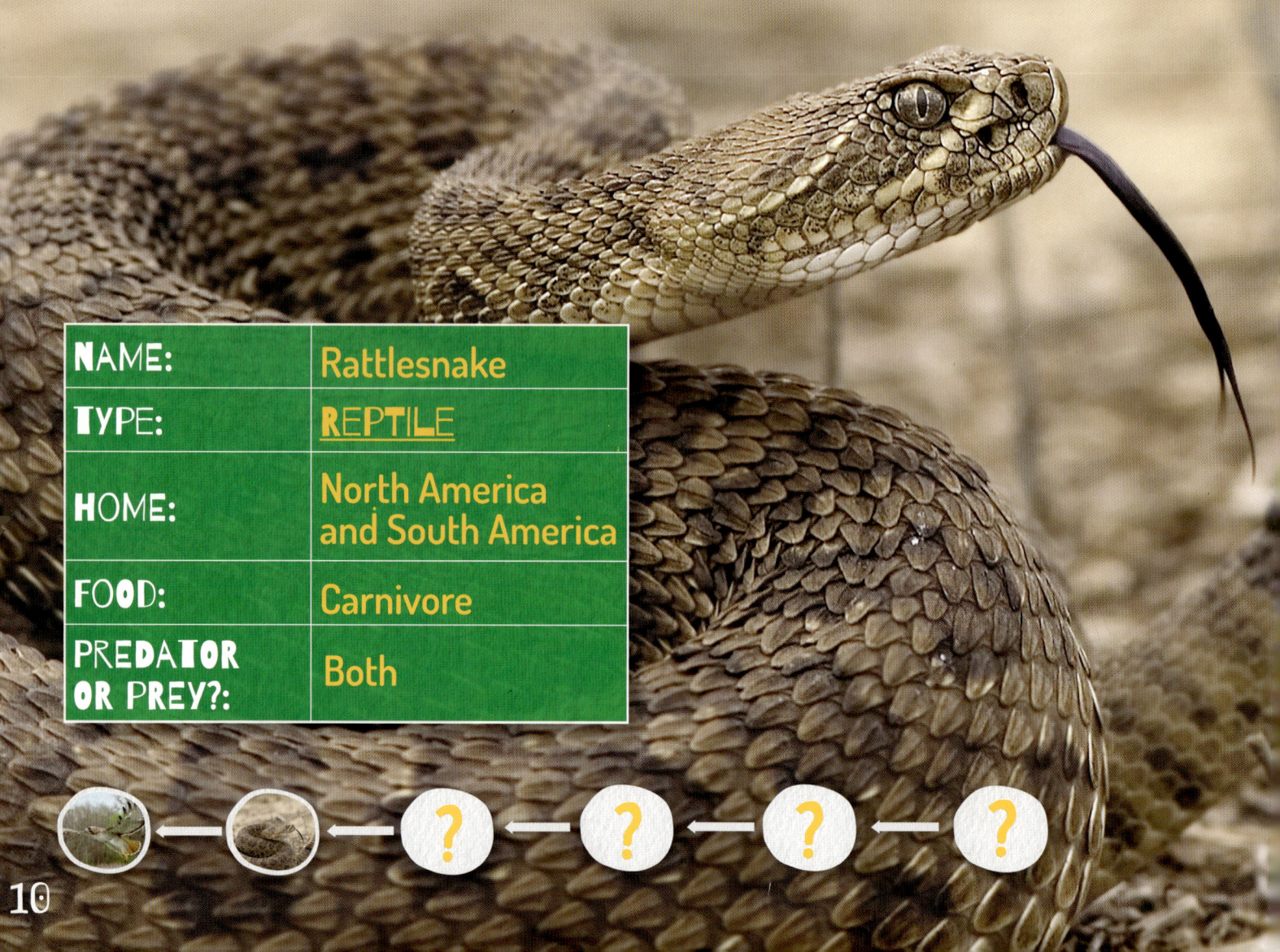

NAME:	Rattlesnake
TYPE:	REPTILE
HOME:	North America and South America
FOOD:	Carnivore
PREDATOR OR PREY?:	Both

Antelope squirrel: cute but yummy…?

Grasshopper: a tasty treat…?

Jackrabbit: a big but brilliant meal…?

It's such a difficult choice. Although I do have a very particular meal in mind…

WHO IS IT?

11

THE KANGAROO RAT

That slithering snake has got a quick bite, but I'm a kangaroo rat and I've got a trick up my furry sleeve. I can jump almost three metres in one bounce to get away from predators!

NAME:	Kangaroo Rat
TYPE:	MAMMAL
HOME:	North America
FOOD:	OMNIVORE
PREDATOR OR PREY?:	Both

Escaping from predators makes me very hungry. I enjoy eating both plants and bugs.

Grasshopper: a jumpy meal...

Cactus longhorn beetle: something with a crunch...

Prickly pear cactus: a spiky dinner...

The grasshopper seems to be a popular choice with the other animals, so maybe I'll give that a try...

HOP AWAY, GRASSHOPPER!

THE GRASSHOPPER

A popular choice? I'm more than popular; everyone seems to want to eat me! Life is difficult as a grasshopper – you have to watch out for predators all the time! All of these animals have tried to catch me for their lunch today...

NAME:	Grasshopper
TYPE:	Insect
HOME:	All Over the World
FOOD:	Herbivore
PREDATOR OR PREY?:	Prey

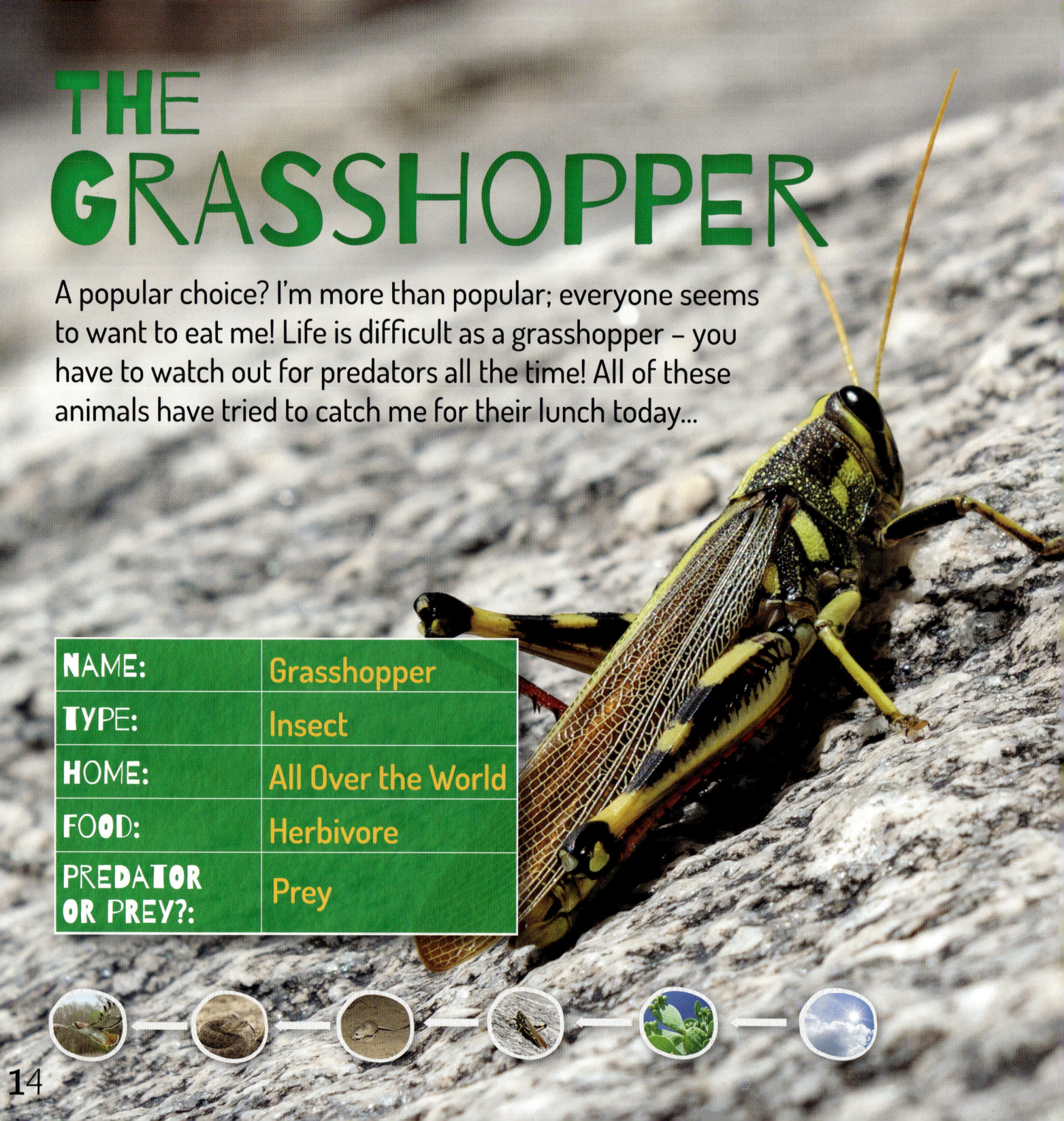

14

Grasshopper mouse: furry and NOT friendly...

Kangaroo rat: jumpy and terrifying...

Rattlesnake: scaly and scary...

But there's one that I'm frightened of more than the others, because it has a big weapon that it's just waiting to catch me with...

WHO COULD IT BE?

15

THE SCORPION

Stay back if you don't want me to attack! I'm a scorpion and I'm very dangerous to be around. No one wants to get close to my stinger – it can give you a very painful sting!

NAME:	Scorpion
TYPE:	ARACHNID
HOME:	All Over the World
FOOD:	Carnivore
PREDATOR OR PREY?:	Prey

I don't eat often. I usually wait until a meal happens to come along. What could be on my menu today?

Cactus longhorn beetle: a spiky snack…?

Grasshopper: a tough catch…?

Other scorpions: a familiar feast…?

My favourite food is other scorpions, but I haven't seen one today. However, there's something else scuttling around nearby…

CAN YOU HEAR IT?

THE CACTUS LONGHORN BEETLE

I certainly hope there aren't any predators hiding around here – I need my meal! I'm a beetle and I like to eat cactus, but so do lots of animals out here in the desert. I hope I get this one all to myself.

NAME:	Cactus Longhorn Beetle
TYPE:	Insect
HOME:	North America
FOOD:	Herbivore
PREDATOR OR PREY?:	Prey

I need to be quick – I'm sure one of these animals will be along for some cactus soon...

Grasshopper mouse: an annoying nibbler...

Jackrabbit: big and bouncy...

Antelope squirrel: sweet but sneaky...

Oh yes! Wonderful news! Something's coming this way that eats all of those animals, but not me...

LET THE FEAST BEGIN! →

THE KIT FOX

Go ahead, little beetle. I'm after something bigger than you for my dinner! I'm a fox and I'm an apex predator in the North American deserts.

NAME:	Kit Fox
TYPE:	Mammal
HOME:	North America
FOOD:	Carnivore
PREDATOR OR PREY?:	Apex Predator

If I wait by this cactus, I'm sure one of these tasty animals will be along shortly... then I can snap them up!

Kangaroo rat: a sweet treat...

Grasshopper mouse: a yummy snack...

Jackrabbit: a hoppy meal...

Antelope squirrel: a furry feast...

21

DESERT FOOD WEB

The arrows follow where the energy goes. Can you follow the energy from the Sun all the way to the hawk and the kit fox?

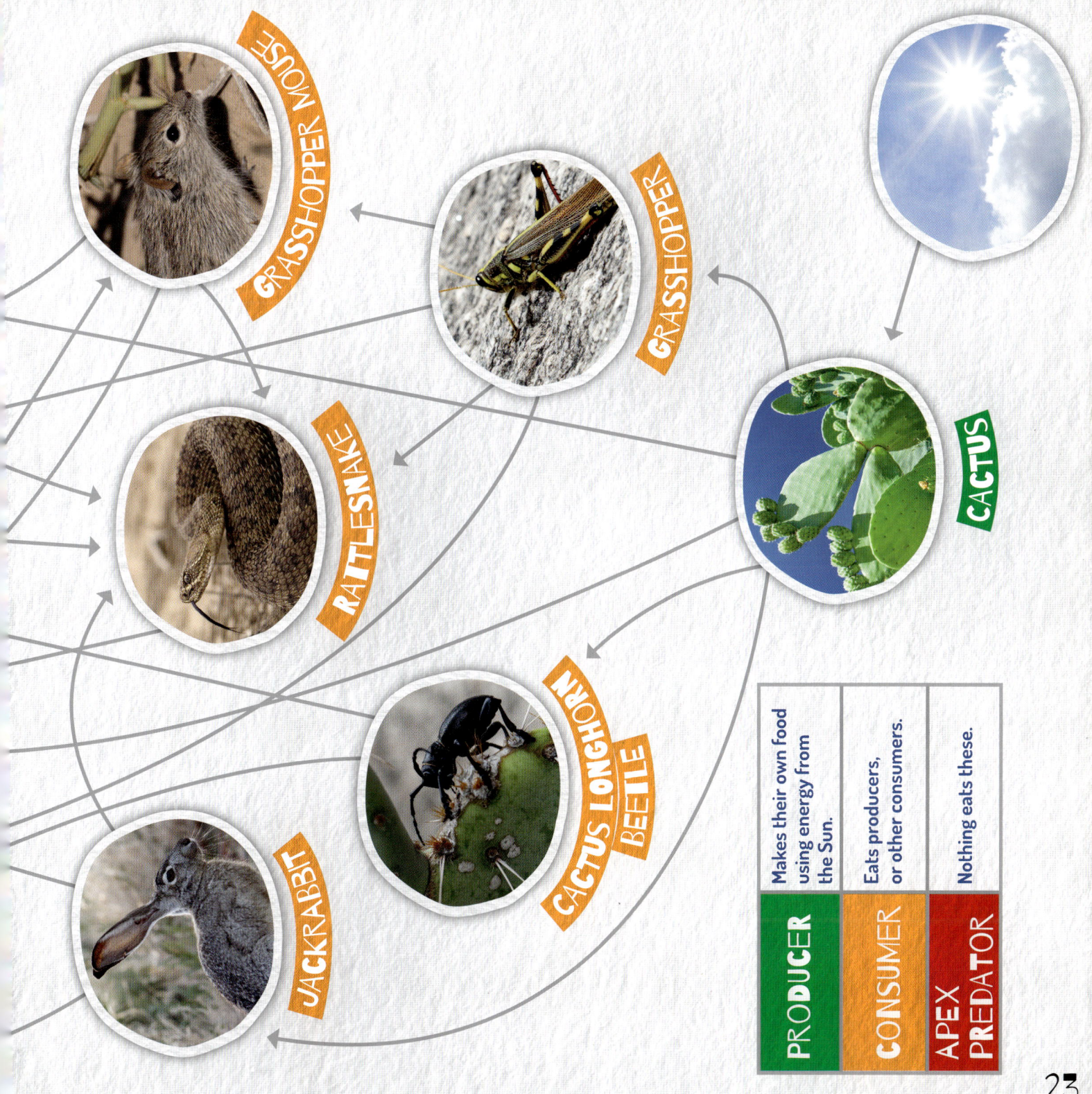

GLOSSARY

apex predators — the top predators in a food chain, with no natural predators of their own

arachnid — a type of animal that has eight legs, such as spiders and scorpions

carnivores — animals that eat other animals, instead of plants

herbivores — animals that eat plants, instead of other animals

mammal — an animal that has warm blood, a backbone and produces milk

omnivores — animals that eat both plants and other animals

predators — animals that hunt other animals for food

prey — animals that are hunted for food

reptile — a cold-blooded animal with scales

INDEX

apex predators 7–8, 10, 20, 22–23
arachnids 16
birds 8
carnivores 7–8, 10, 16, 20
herbivores 6–7, 14, 18
insects 14, 18
mammals 12, 20
North America 5, 8, 10, 12, 18, 20
omnivores 12
reptiles 10
South America 10